SACRED WOUNDS

PW COVINGTON

PRAISE FOR PW COVINGTON

In an age of volunteer military forces, PW's words paint the line between those who serve and those who do not. For those who've worn the uniform, his stories about war read like lullabies.

- **Sara Sneath**, USMC veteran and environment reporter, *The Victoria Advocate*

PW Covington's newest poetry collection, <u>Sacred Wounds</u>, is forceful and in-your-face.

These poems do not let you sit in complacency and apathy; they make you take a look at your surroundings and realize it's not too late to become part of the solution.

Covington smacks you around with truth about depthless patriotism, TV-driven consumer culture and PTSD among our veterans; then, he gives a short reprieve with a reflective moment on the road or a quiet morning reading in a hotel room before resuming the poetic smack-down.

Taking the reader along on his deployments, his travels, his stints behind bars, and his poetry tours, Covington entertains with his beatnik witticisms and flowing meter, while educating on the gritty realities of life in the military contrasted with life in small-town Texas.

This book should be read by anyone who needs to be shaken out of their comfort zone and given a fresh dose of raw truth.

-Lilly Penhall, Author and Editor,
Penhall Publishing

These poems by veteran and neo-Beat poet PW Covington strike a chord with me, even though I've never served. His writing is very masculine but sensitive, a throwback to another type of male, another type of writer.

Male writers today are either all too weepy-sensitive or they're trying their student-best to be some macho man that doesn't exist anymore. The power and profound emotions his poems evoked turned me on to a new American poet.

-**Ezekiel Tyrus**
The Beat Museum, San Francisco,
Author; **Eli, Ely, Hardhead Press**

SACRED WOUNDS

PW COVINGTON

SLOUGH PRESS

Edited by Dr. Charles Taylor Jr., PhD.

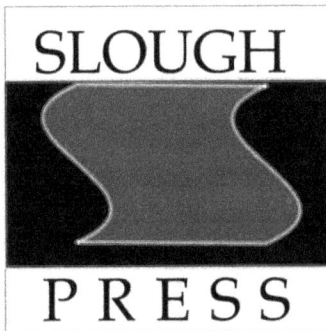

SLOUGH

S

PRESS

www.sloughpressbooks.com

SLOUGH PRESS
ISBN: 978-0-941720-42-7

Alamo and Kyle, Texas

Cover Art taken from an original painting by Corina Carmona

I *dedicate this book to…*

every artist that has ever traded hours of highway for seconds of applause.

every writer that has ever lost their mind but found their voice.

every wayfarer, every dreamer, every volunteer out in the night.

I dedicate this book to…

imprisoned poets.

artists in uniform.

tutors, teachers, and mentors.

I dedicate this book to…

the light at the end of the tunnel, and to the darkness within.

-PWC

Family Housing

I was born near the end of the runways
On a Cold War, California
Desert Air Force Base
Phantom jets and F-105's
Thundered overhead, and I slept as a
    baby
Secure in my bed

Clean, small, communities with familiar
    paces
Retreat played every afternoon

We stood up for our flag

We'd ride our BX bikes anywhere,
Pretending they were sleek, fighter planes
In family housing

New schools, every two or three years
That clean, small town was movable,
Interchangeable
Safe

"Brat" was an endearing term
We wore it with pride, like uniforms, like
    decoration

Still, today, sometimes
Life seems to make more sense
The other side of the "100% ID check,
Deadly Force Authorized" signs

Where we all drive slow, in four door
    cars,
And pickup trucks
Through
Family housing

Where everything still stops
For those bugles at the end of the duty
    day

Where jet noise or turbo prop drone
Does not scream "War" to me,

But whispers of home

Don't Give it a Name

It's more deniable when it doesn't have a
    name
All you see, all you can hold, are pieces
    of the facts
It can be hard to speak of it at all
If you just don't give it a name

But since we were small, there has been a
    tug to define, To label, to contain
To find, to validate
Within the lines
Even the dead, to be truly mourned, need
    names

It is easier to live through it all when they
    don't have names
It is easier to kill, when you don't have a
    name
And, when all you pick up from the crater
    in the road at the checkpoint

Are pieces of the facts-
Hands and legs and blood soaked debris
You pray and pray that you don't find a
    name

When blood and waste and hell and fire
    are the world you live in,
The thousands of miles to your rear can
    whisper
That it is all temporal and all evil and that
    you are…
And playing the same role…

That you've seen all the faces a spirit can
    hold

The cold, burning, truth doesn't matter-
Won't matter, anymore
Teeth and hair, an ear, skull fragments in
    grey
Do not make a face, do not have a name

Just shut up about who you THINK
    this was
It can't have a name, if the task is to be

    done
When the time is right, at the end of some
    flight,
They'll give it one
Long after you and I are done

When our names, too, may be swallowed
    by our stories
Our history
Our sinking sun

(For M.N.)

Indirect Fire

When rockets or mortars, third-world
artillery, fall while you sleep

It is called indirect fire

200, 300 meters away

Or, maybe, right next door

You are told to think nothing of it

And

In time, you, too, are joking

Trying not to sound like a

Fear-filled Fobbit

Never admit your humanity

Around those facing more present,
better-aimed dangers

Farther downrange

Indirect fire makes you lucky,
   they'll say

But New Years and July 4

Are never the same

Indirect fire can be laughed away

Until you report to the airfield the
   next day

And load metal transfer cases

Onto large, grey, planes

And when you learn the names of

Two American Service members
killed last night

From the shipping documents,
coded for Dover,

Before the news, before their
families

It does not seem

Very

Indirect

At all

DeWitt County

Rusting, metal, windmill fans and Co-op
    power poles
Are the highest points for miles around
Mesquite, scrub oak, and huisache,
Graze the plains like one thorny herd,
Clinging to the greenness of late Spring

The cattle are not native, but like many
    here, they've shaped the land
This Earth gives witness to commerce
    and beasts
The Longhorn, Brangus, and
Santa Getrudis, straight off the King
Ranch
Coyotes, jackrabbits, and armadillos are
    aboriginal South Texans,
 They guard unmarked Comanche tombs,
    and keep the secrets of the Karankawa

The odd-pump-jack bobs slowly up and
down….up…and down
  bowing to a long, gone, shallow sea
Under the timeless sun, blazing in early
Summer
You find a shed copperhead skin,
bleached and wrapped around a cistern
    pipe
A cast-off reminder of gradual change

…and the passions of reptiles

Breathe in that air; that thick, warm,
    potable, air
Let it into the ear of your soul
Hay sol, hay humedad,
Listen to the tarantula, listen to the
    horned toad, listen to the caracara
Look to the cottontail and to the

mapache, the cottonmouth and the
bobcat
Find the tracks made by mules and burros
that first brought churches and trails.

Brown Eyes

A lonely, brown-eyed child appears,
She clutches a Disney doll
And petitions me

With the eyes of Mogadishu
The eyes of Matagalpa

The eyes of Matamoros

Eyes too dry to cry
Eyes too tired to hope for more

Than survival

Short Final (Somalia 1992-93)

How old were you in 1992?
I was 18, and I was not an infantryman
At Christmas time I flew to war
On Comet, on Cupid, on Donner, and
    blitzed in
... into Mogadishu on a Hercules
I was not an infantryman

News cameras and equatorial black faces
    swarmed us at the airport
Chanting, USA! USA!

At night, mortars would fall
Shaking the ruined walls we reclined
    behind,
Death, daring us to sleep
Always the shit-smell of the air
Would hang visible on short final
Short final - about to hit ground
In 1992 I was 18
And I was not an infantryman

That place couldn't keep up with all the
    death I saw

Bodies would lay atop each other in the
    streets,
Along with camels and dogs,
And brass shell casings and spent RPG
    tubes
It would percolate and boil and bake and
    steam,
And sometimes explode
We'd scramble for cover
I was not an infantryman

I was not an infantryman,
Any killing that I did
Came later
In a bottle,
In a letter,
In a whorehouse,
In a thousand ways,
Thousands of miles away
After friend and foe,
Lover and stranger,
Right and wrong and Jesus Christ
Just didn't matter anymore.

I was not an infantryman
I didn't get to fire back
When sniper fire would shatter the ramp
    concrete into powder at our heels
As we worked to offload the tools of
    conflict
Or upload the injured and the dead...the
    only spoils of war I ever saw, but...
I was not an infantryman

That little war of my youth
    gets lost, over looked
Between the faded flag confetti of so
    called desert Victory
And this current sticky mire
I'm left to soldier on

But I am not an infantryman
And short, short final
Can last for decades
Like a freefall of free-floating detachment
Still airborne
Still hanging somewhere over East Africa
A mist of useless, irrelevant, dismissed
    regret

Just a few colored ribbons to my name
I have nothing heroic to tell you about

I was not an infantryman

It Was Not Sacrifice

When you see the flag wave
And you drive past the graves
Dug into the land of the Free
At the homes of the Brave
When the battle-tanks roar
Or the jet-bombers soar
Do you really know what the
Fighting is for?

So, have your parades
On those July days
And your flags; you can raise 'em
    and think yourself right

…to talk of sacrifice…

But, you'd be mistaken

They did not fade away-
They were murdered and slain
Their lives were taken

They were scared and shaking-
Tired and quaking

Fighting only to…
Make it through

With the only dream
To just keep living
It was not sacrifice-

That was not how they died
(Not even the brave ones)

They died for their Brothers and Pride,
Once all they could do was die;
It was never willing
War is crime and war is a lie

And war is only killing

Shrapnel and steel can not cut a deal
For progress or reason

Jesus and King
Don't mean a God-damned thing
In the havoc and mayhem

So don't call it heresy
And don't call it treason
It was simply killing

Wake from restful dreams and
Secure lives
Foundations unshaken
And reap the rewards
From those that knew war
And will never awaken

Have your parades
On those November days
And in the rockets' red glare
You can look to the air

And speak with duty and trite
Of their 'sacrifice'

…But you'd be mistaken
It was no sacrifice

Their lives were taken

The Last Time that the World Ended

The last time that the world ended, I was
   there
 We rushed in like Angels
 They let me be an angel, the last time
   that the world ended.

It was the worst storm,
The strongest twister,
The biggest fire,
The most noble war.
And we tried, we tried...
 To pull innocence from the twisted
   rubble,
 We brought people off of roofs.
 There were army rations and Red Cross
   cots
  And visits from Presidents and
   governors

We searched house to house,
 Removed fallen trees from post-storm
   streets

Spray painted X's on front doors as each
    home was cleared
No expense was spared, the last time that
    the world ended

New Orleans, Texas, New York City
Alabama, Mississippi, New Orleans again

Disaster becomes only a word after too
    long
And grief always looks the same from the
    sky

When every storm is the worst storm

How many times have I rebuilt my life?
How much destroyed or left behind,
    by forces of nature, by acts of God, by
Mindlessness and happenstance?
Where were the legions of angels, then?

So, this time, I will not run into the
    disaster,

The stars do not call to me personally
Anymore, for they have been told to be
Wary of my weariness
   I am no longer on the roster of
Super heroes, now that my own disasters
     have been shared.
I will not look into loss-filled eyes this
     time.
I will not know the stench of human
     decay in sun-drenched suburbs.
There will be no reassurances, no
     comforting, no glorious god-less faith
     in man...

How close is too close to stand,
 The next time the world decides to end?

Victoria, Texas… Subterranean

The men in the churches
 Should not be trusted
Have you heard what they are praying
   for?

The soldiers and sailors
 Should not be thanked
Do you know what they have done?

The police of this city
 Should not be obeyed
Have you heard what they're being
   trained to do to us?

Words like Faith and Family
 Are weapons in this town
Greed and Hate and Fear abound

Hope is here, though
It wears black
It drinks, it smokes, it fucks
It falls asleep on broken glass
And wakes up with jagged cuts
It lays down with ringing ears
And inhales shale oil vapors
Hope, here, dreams nightmarish shit
That never makes the papers

Don't trust the men in churches
 You're better off with whores
Jesus, the Beatnik Nazarene
Taught us this before

And before you thank a soldier
Learn exactly what he did…
Did he ass-rape captured fighters, or
rescue injured kids?

It's not even getting better
Not around here

So fuck your halls of higher learning

  And fuck your Red

Your White

Your Blue

And, fuck your dollar, too
And fuck the fact that fuck is the
Only fucking word that's true

Stuff your fetid, fatted, face
While others starve and weep

Obey, obey, obey

The wolves
You pay to patrol your streets

The red is blood and green is wealth
And virgins don't give birth

The miracles are underground
For any good they're worth

They bury us
Subterraneans

Beneath hate and fear and war
They come for us, in light of day
In armored police cars

Though we fight, and though we rail
We never find a way
To rise up from the underground
Like seeds to light of day

Decay

The men in the churches

The men in the churches

The Smoke Also Rises...

Why do the conspiratorial giggles
Of teenage girls at the bookstore
Make me long for machine gun fire
And strong black tea?

And what of all those precious, beloved,
infants of American inheritance?
Held tighter to their mothers' chests
When they pass me on the street,
And I know exactly how far the blood
    would flow
If I were to grab that tender package...
So unique, so special
The mixing of zygotes and lustful urges,
If I were to grab it by its ankles,
And swing it, head first, into the red brick
    wall
Beside me,
What of it that I know exactly how far the
    blood would flow?

Cigarette smoke rises on the breeze from
     a table of
Affectedly disaffected young women
Black hair dye and nail polish
Cell phones and talk of online
     communiqués

The smoke also rises from the ruins of a
     minaret
While golden-mocha boys in green T-
     shirts
Point plastic Klanishnakovs at me and
     smile

And those damned,
Those God-damned stickers and magnets
Posted so close to car trunks stuffed fat
     with
Useless, plastic, Holiday crap
Save the bumper stickers for your honor
     student

I guess a magnetic ribbon...made in China
Is the next best thing to actually fighting
     yourself

Why do Low-impact patriotism
And carefully measured sentiment
Make me hear mortar fire and sirens
And the screams of faceless Marine
  riflemen?

Tell Me

(for Jason C.)

Tell Me
Tell Me
Tell Me
About me
Brother, No one else is gonna listen to
    you
No one else is gonna give you the time
    that you wrestle from me
And repeating lies, time after time, still
    don't make them true
Dude!

Tell me how I've never worked a day

(Never a day loading planes, nor a day at
sea, nor a day driving a truck, nor a day
working steel, nor a shift behind a
microphone, nor a night on a stage....I've
never known a warehouse, nor a pasture,
nor a desk...never submitted a manuscript

soaked in hunger to get back a toilet
paper roll of rejection letters)

Tell me how I've scammed EVERYONE
I have ever known
Tell me these things-These truths-Known
    only to you
Tell me these things, and then just go
    away
(Or stay)
Leave me alone
Leave me alone

Alone-like those nights on the streets of
San Francisco and El Paso
Alone- like in a prison cell in Texas
Alone- like in the State Hospital, or in a
    hundred other places along the way
...Never worked a day, you say?

I looked around when my feet hit the
    ground
After the storm,

After the flood,
After the fire
I looked around when I hit the ground
When the rifles' sound turned me around
And I looked in the faces of my Brothers-
You weren't there
Tell me
Tell me
Tell me
Where were you?

Maybe you were in a church somewhere
Or staring in a mirror, combing your hair
For 20 years, I looked around and
You
Weren't
There

So, tell me these things you claim are true
But, spare me your plans...
No.
Tell me them, too

Then go back and do the things that you
    do

Home Owners' Club. Mega-Church
 Idol-nation
Child-rearing lifestyle,
Inheritance Greed,
Sibling Harassment and Investigation
(North Houston suburban frustration)

Tell me
Tell me
Tell me

How the heavy axe of finance
Swings right at your neck
And, how to work is to sweat,
How the sweat of your brow
Makes you better somehow...?
It's all Financed Wealth...
A share-cropped cash cow.
Wow!

Tell me
Tell me

Tell me, Brother

Where is the freedom in your life?
Beyond your heirs, beyond your wife?
Beyond wrong, beyond right?

If tomorrow you woke up
In a Tucson train yard
With no credit cards,
With nothing but a rumble in your
    stomach
And a couple dozen warrants,
And an eye swollen shut from last night's
    bum-rush.
Could you find your way,
When even Jesus wouldn't give you the
    time of day?
(Could you even LIVE life MY way?)
Say!

Say whatever you gotta say-
I ain't tryin' to shut you up
I ain't tryin' to bust your gig-
You're living the way you choose to live
But,
Can you dig?

I've made my set of choices, too
Not all for the best; true, true
But, I've never let a dollar bill
Define for me what is real
And I have never ONCE let "Jesus take
the wheel"

Tell me
Tell me
Tell me
Tell me about me, Brother

No one else is gonna listen to you
No one else is gonna lend you the time
that I do
And repeating those lies STILL don't
make them true
And I know you'll hate anything that I do

But, go ahead....Tell me-

I'll always be here for you

Recidivists

Does it make you feel noble,

There at the bar, with all the other
White-collared, white-washed,
     conspiratorial smiles?
Do you feel pride and purpose?

Was law school worth it?
Serving up penal punishment like cold,
     bologna sandwiches
Are you content in the evening, with
     justice and Jesus?
 Or, is it just a job to you?

I've been here before

Shit,

Not free for 60 days

Already back to my criminal ways.
We keep shooting the same scene,

Playing the same roles,
Using the same script,
Slamming those same doors.

Statistically, I knew I'd be back again.
And that you'd still sit there, with that
same white-bread grin.

Your prison worked so well the first time,

Ferguson Unit, red-bricked, dog-pound
What could be different, this time down?

Dominguez Unit, State Jail-bound.

16 months to wonder how.

RECIDIVIST – State Pen
Texas, ape-shit, off the deep end.

What about that coveted
    "accountability"?
Christian, pick-up truck, judges and

juries?
What a waste, if you never "reformed"
  me.

Rehabilitation went out (when)
The needle came back (in)

Redemption contingent on a background
  check
Is it any wonder that there is no respect in
  me left
For all you hold sacred, for all you
  believe
When all it ever came down to was
  double-fuck ME?

Find something new.

What can you do when the truth
No longer proves true?
As I sign my plea, we see the same thing
Recidivists, slithering back here again

So, I'll sign on the line.

I'll retreat in my mind,
To the terrible places that you'll never
    find
  (until the next time)

When, we will gather together, with roles
    well rehearsed
You'll know my lines, and I'll know
    yours.

Recidivists.

PTSD

PTSD
Put This Shit Down
Put it down on paper
Read it aloud
Let it see the light of day
Show those that weren't there
What was there
What is there

The truth is horrible
But never as malevolent as lies and
    secrets
Lies and Secrets started this in the first
    place

PTSD
Put This Shit Down
Put it down,
So that it's there
Somewhere tangible
In lines
On paper

In a little book
Up on a shelf
So that it's not just loitering in my mind-
Like a gunship
Banking slowly to the left...

PTSD
Put This Shit Down
Put this shit down, Doctor-
I've killed because I was just too tired to
    care
Too scared to scream,
Too numb for morality or reality to
    matter much

Put this shit down...
And tell me, if my sentence…
This life…
Fits my crime

And talk to me of peace
If that's what's on your mind,
And you can put things down that you've
    never experienced...
I'll allow that-

Because I do understand
The need we all have to

Put This Shit Down

Written While Volunteering at the Homeless Shelter Where I Once Slept

True
Buddhas'
Saints' and Gods'
Snores are sutras
From green army cots
Away, in these mangers

Snores
Echo
Down the hall
Of the shelter
Open freezing nights
For those with no place else

Hot
Coffee

Folding chairs
Fluorescent lights
Rolling Cigarettes
Against Insomnia

Poems that Begin with the Letter "I"

I am guilty
I am included
I am crybaby, lecherous, disability
welfare, pot smoker

Unreliable

I am victim, attacker, liar and clown

I am a thief, a scoundrel
A saint
I am praying
A folly
A collection of myths in the morning
    twilight
False dawn

The cork out of an absinthe bottle
I am slum lord of this Texas imagination

All these poems that begin with the letter
"I"

Veterans Assistance Office (4-27-2004)

Yesterday I sat in the Veterans Assistance
Office
On the TV it was live...
In green night-vision tones
The Marine Corps launched a new
    offensive
On the city of Fallujah

...Just another foreign city's name
Those kids will never forget
Like my own bloodstained travelogue:

BIADOWA KISMAAYO BASRA AL-
TIAF MOGADISHU

10 years after I slid back stateside,
Like a defanged adder
Into the wide-closed arms of an America
    with
More important things on its picture-tube
    mind
Sitting..in the Veterans Assistance Office

Little wars..............We were so BIG
God's own Giants, Chocolate-chipped
Titans with carbines
Avenging Angels with gunship support
Infidels with Ammunition and Armored
Chariots

Sent to places we'd never heard of in
    small town high schools

The GI Joe dolls would once fit neatly
back into the toy chest at the end of the
    war
In 10 years, how many will sit in the
Veterans Assistance Office?
Who picks up these toys..broken,
    discarded...now,

After Fallujah...?
After Mogadishu...

When the toothless dogs of war flop
    down
Into the cushioned green seats
Of the Veterans Assistance Office?

Veterans Assistance Office (Sequel, 2014)

Today,
 I am volunteering at the Veterans
Assistance Office
I have not watched television in years
Every day the view gets a bit more clear

A young man, with a back pack, and a
    two week beard
Has just told me about
Things that happened in Fallujah.

A place he has tried
To leave behind
A place that no one he knows

Can understand, at least no one he could
    find
Until…the Veterans Assistance Office

VICTORIA CUERO PORT LAVACA

even AUSTIN HOUSTON SAN
ANTONIO

His war, our wars
Did not suddenly end, just by coming
    home

10 years; a decade

Seems about right

To learn to heal, after learning to fight
To learn that you do not
Need to stay a serpent
Because you once had fangs
I have shed that skin (and)

Today, I work in the
Veterans Assistance Office

No war is little
No war is noble
No hero's life is pure or true
God does not wave flags
    or tally score

When soldiers do as they must do

And small towns can be battle zones
Once you are done with medals and dress
    blues

And, the cadence can still echo across the
    years
As hope sprouts from war-borne tears,
We help each other up

After Fallujah,
After Mogadishu

When we no longer

See the need to feed
The feeble hounds of war

When guns, and rank, and uniforms
No longer keep us warm

Ode to a Corduroy Coat

I don't remember, for sure,
Just where I got this coat
This brown sport coat
This corduroy jacket
But, it might have been a South Austin
thrift store in mid-Spring

It's a little ratty, a little worn
But the sleeves are long enough
And it's not too warm
This corduroy jacket;
Together, we've committed countless acts
    of poetry
From McAllen to Salt Lake City

This corduroy jacket is street-wise;
It's seen the French Quarter

I left it behind once

After a night of 3-way, power-exchange,
    sex
In a hotel room not far from the airport in
San Antonio
But, it came back to me, the following
    week
Like something real and lasting
After the scent and sting of lust had gone

  This corduroy jacket does not have suede
    patches on the sleeves

This corduroy jacket is a college drop-out
And, it is used to staying crumpled,
    behind a car seat, for months at a time
This corduroy jacket is my poetry - it fits
    me

  It's got strange, hidden, inside pockets
It is out of place in Texas

  I have other coats, but I wear it most

A favorite, sacred shield,
I wear it like safety gear
The full armor of my appetites
This corduroy jacket
Fits me, follows me, finds me
My wayward haberdashery
This corduroy jacket still has poems to
    tell and nights to welcome home

.

Breaking Up with Jimmy Buffett

Jimmy Buffett broke up with me last night, in my dream.

As we were leaving his place, he pulled me aside and told me, "When you get home, don't ever contact me again", which was kind of a shame, because my girlfriend seemed to be getting along so well with his mother, who looked like her mother, in my dream.

I guess, looking back, I had seen it coming for decades. How he was a no show at a Katrina benefit, playing a corporate gig for Tyco executives that night instead. The branding – tequila, beer, casual dining theme restaurants. Lawsuits, claiming trademark infringement whenever the word "Margarita" and an image of a parrot appeared together.

A long, long, way from living in the back of Jerry Jeff Walker's car and smoking weed and doing lines with Ann Richards on the south shore of Town Lake.

We'll always have A1A, and Down to Earth, and ¾ Time. In every latitude, there are attitudes that just don't stay the same, when money enters the food chain; rhythms that no longer rhyme. Even in Lower Alabama, even in Florida. No, he didn't owe me anything, I just kind of found him when I needed an excuse for Post-Catholic, Aero-obsessed, over-literate, salt water, don't-give-a-fuck.

But, sooner or later, we all grow into our family names, like it or not.

The last time I saw him in Texas, there

were one hour lines for watered down boat drinks. There were $45 Tshirts that I'd never wear in public. Private, logo'ed enclaves, all over the amphitheater grounds, offered air conditioning for $100 up-charges.

I have never been comfortable in large crowds of suburban white people. Frat boys and FOX blondes, all grown up now, with sitters for the night and Tommy Bahama beachwear.

There will be no more Deaths of Unpopular Poets, and the Coconut Telegraph never really synched to digital.

Goodbye, Jimmy Buffett. I have sunsets to seek, poems to find, and tides to ride. You owe me nothing, and it's better this way.

Really, It's not you; it's me. I have found my own wings; my own sails have filled.

Reading Up on Ecuador

Pilgrims still seek these shores
But, I'm reading up on Ecuador
With a dog and a cat at my feet
Out on my Texas porch

It's a sunny, winter, day
Like the houseplants,
I've pulled myself outside for sun
Waiting for Kerouac to amble up my
    street

We'll swap stories about
Ships and Disability benefits; VA
    hospitals and riding in stolen cars
We will not speak of poetry
And I will not share my wine

I'm reading up on Ecuador
They say it's easy living
In a land that isn't yours

Freed from all responsibility

To fix, to clean up, to plant, to teach
No need to sweat, or serve, or toil, or
    bleed
The expatriate life;
Behind doors, Behind walls, Behind gates
Down streets with signs printed in
English
Antiseptic isolation

A life of Yankee leisure

What would Wm. Burroughs do?

The Rio Grande Valley still looks great
This time of year
Palm Trees, Palm Trees
10th street in McAllen
It runs on, and on, and on

God bless them, God bless them
With the Beatest prayer I ever learned

As it was in the beginning, Is now, And
    ever will be

I'm reading up on Ecuador

The Zen of Nowhere

The Zen of this place
Is nowhere

The Zen of nowhere
Is now

The Zen of a window is win
The Zen of a door is do

Zendo

Which door
From the multitude
Do you choose
To walk through

To chase Zen?

The Zen of the chase

Leads to nowhere

The Zen of nowhere
 is Now

Never Work with Food
(Field Workers in California)

It is still about field workers in California

But, it's also about fast food employees in
Texas

And packing plant laborers in Kansas

Dogs, treated with more dignity
Than those that manufacture
Supermarket brand pet foods
It isn't always about food

Not always
But, food is a damned good place to start
Thinking about the 21st century
Wage Slave

The red in Red State Union busting
Is the blood leaking onto our dinner

platter
The Fire sauce at Taco Bell,
It polishes the floors at
The Whole Foods corporate office in
   Texas
In dirty slaughter house jeans or
Pressed Wall-Mart Street suits,
The stench is the same

It is still about field workers in California
Suffering and inequality are the
Diet of this nation

Hate and fear, served for 99 cents
In a paper wrapper
White, male, privilege on the table
Every Sunday, after church

Where, we are taught to be prosperous;

That, to be successful, means

To never work with food.

Hemlock

This evening,
I am ordering hemlock
Over ice
In a rocks glass
From the bar at the hotel
Compromising with the barman,
Agave will do

Poisoning myself with south Texas
With denial
With faith and flags and family
I am poisoning myself with poetry
Poisoning myself with the
Cheap highway stuff, 87 octane
Poisoning myself with
The company of women
That I will never fuck

I'm not even sure what mirrors are for

Anymore
Poisoning myself with vanity
Sweet, sweet pride in mid-Spring swelter
This is not New England
Poisoning myself on promises
Made decades ago
On other continents

I am poisoning myself with the patience

Of a snake tail rattling
Poisoning myself with cheap, counter-
    top, condiments
With vending machine ice
At the Echo Hotel
I am poisoning myself with walls
And rifles…And checkpoints

Surveillance blimps tethered with

Long
White
Cords

I am poisoning myself like a peacock,
Shooting the Rio Grande River
Into rolling, shy, veins
A bump of smack backstage
Then on with the show
Tonight, I am feeling familiar, forgotten
Untrusted

I am poisoning myself with embossed
credit cards
Transfixed by my name pressed on
plastic
Poisoning myself on the streets of Austin
Somewhere south of the river
And north of Ben White
I am poisoning myself on Craigslist

Sucking cocks in a

Zilker Park restroom

I am poisoning myself, looking for Venus
Through Army-surplus binoculars
In an era of
Don't ask
Don't tell
Don't share
I don't know

I am poisoning myself with muddy
Houston steam
And in smoky backrooms in Dallas
Poisoning myself with passions and
    dreams
Lessons and schemes
With poems written on napkins
Like plea-bargains

Trees shed leaves and serpents
Slough skin

It's in places like this, I poison myself
Kill off
What does not belong
Gun stores and tequila
Offend me

But, I'll drink with you

All
Night
Long.

A Few Grains of Sand

There is still sand in my fists
A few grains there I feel
Now and again

A few grains of sand from a far desert
    land
That I feel in my fists
Every now and again

That I feel in the fists that I shake
At all that I am
Since making back from that far, desert
    land

And I wish that somehow I could fly
Across oceans again
And let blood wash my hands
Of these few grains of sand

Grains that I feel when I clench my fists
When I clench my fists
Every now and again

As I shake them high at all I have been
And I spit at and yearn for that far, desert
    land
I curse and crave the grains in my hand

The few grains I feel, now and again
That I feel in my fists
From a far, desert land

For Edward Vidaurre

I went to sleep last night
　　and I did not dream
I did not sweat or heave
　　nor wrestle with my self
My dissatisfaction, my hunger, my guilt
I did not scream
When I awoke

Edward is reading
Ferlinghetti in the Valley
If there is hope,
Hope is there
For a decade after the "good war",
　　the right war, the big war
Dreamers dreamed, writers wrote,
　　and poetry was a physical force

I woke up and took a photograph
　　at a Memorial Day parade-
I used a "retro-wash" filter, and posted it
　　online...

Where is OUR beat movement?
Who are OUR subterranean,
Bodhisattva mujaheddin
What about OUR hitchhike highway,
Reform school, Benzedrine,
Pistol-packing poets?

After 20 years of war,
   is all we are capable of
Idealization and celebration?

Always looking back
   to artists that dared demand change in
The world?
   Change in themselves?

DON'T study "The Beats",
   BE BEAT......No, just BE!

Don't talk to me about Cassady
Don't read me Negro Streets at Dawn;
Write me from dingy Texas jail cells,

Share with me your weed, your pills,
Your mescaline
Can you even find a bottle of
 Absinthe in this town?

Dream and wake and write and fuck and
    cry
Kill something major,
Leave your truest love forsaken,
    prove nothing,
 Live naked and on fire.
Avoid classrooms, spend decades
Drunk in border-town dive bars,
    in railway cars, in wooded fields
    alone.

When did I forget how to dream?
When did hunger turn to irony?

Echo Hotel

The Echo Hotel echoes the faint
    Beat leftovers
Of rattlesnakes and Benzedrine
I am the inhaler of moist,
    borderland air
With the hair of the dog on a
    morning of words
That will stretch from Pharr to San
Benito
But I am not an adding machine
    heir
No MFA, No PhD, no, no...

It took a hurricane and 38 years to
    get me to New York City
But, I know the road
And I've been through St. Louis,

And Mexico, too
The Rio Grande Valley is still a
    great place to lay low
With just a little more concrete
And a few more questions
Than old Bull ever had to negotiate
Sooner or later we all get killed by
The lions
Like good Christians should

These echoes I hear in
Room 508

 From somewhere off in the
    direction
    of the golf course out back...

Ambrose

Your middle name was Ambrose
I never knew that
Until I read it in the Cuero Record
    obituary
Lifelong rancher, the newspaper said
No mention of those cut-throat early
    years
Working South Texas oil rigs
From Edinburg to Laredo
Like "Giant", but no cinema-scope
1st generation Polack American- As was
    your wife of 56 years

Everyone in DeWitt County learned to
pronounce the name "Dlugosch"
The bankers and deed clerks learned to
    spell it, too

That ancient, black, vinyl, living room
    chair...next to the front door, with a
 Rifle behind it
Dearborn heater, butane.....no air
    conditioning
You died as the first Northern winds of
    the season
Made their way down to Mesquite brush
    country

I remember tobacco- Levi Garrett from a
    tan pouch
I remember a spittoon that had once been
    a Folgers can
And the smell of burnt, percolated coffee,
Even on 100 degree afternoons, from the
    old, linoleum kitchen
Deer sausage in the Winter,

Until I got too old, too busy, too
    travelled,
Too shamed

To travel those red-dirt, gravel roads to
    visit you

You died with your boots on
And wearing Dickies Pants
Behind the wheel of a parked pick-up
Out on Tekla's old place
-Checking on cows
Cows that were to be shipped the next
    day
You knew the end was coming

I remember rural childhood Summers
A month or so away from my young
    parents.
On Sunday mornings,
You didn't have to ride with Grandma
To the big Catholic Church in town
Where St. Michael fought the demon
And where Heaven and Hell
And Priests and Nuns
And things only whispered about, dwelt

Ironic, now, that I will be carrying you
With four other grandsons;
Me-

The only one never to have worked the
    oil field
The only one never to have worked cattle
Me- with the English last name
Into that same church

To an altar I last visited on the morning
    of my
Holy Confirmation
And tonight I am missing the strong, full,
    sweet taste of Levi Garrett

As I Watched the Flags Being Put Away at the End of the Business Day (9/11/2013)

Wrap

Yourself

In the flag

And invoke God

Of your own image,

With shared hatreds and fears

When

You Pray

Be sure to

Remember that

You chose to keep

Profits over service

Wave;

It's not

Your Red blood,

Not your Blue heart,

In symmetrical

White cemetery rows

Bukowski for Breakfast in Corpus Christi

Cheap motel morning

100 miles away from home,
Last night's homicide scene out the back
    window

No in-room coffee pot, just CNN and the
    local TV news

I shut it off.

And read Bukowski for breakfast

Catching a Cab from 26th and Valencia

They called for a cab from 26th and
Valencia
To the Whitcomb Hotel,
Market Street, Civic Center
Some word misplaced
One too many Mission Street drinks
It was their first trip, together, out west

With power-exchange yearning
In her dark, leather, eyes
He, still clinging to
A façade of masculine pride

The next time through such
Heavy, wooden doors,
She would lead
And, with an exhaled breath and
An unburdened peace
He would follow her, humbled, yet
    majestic

But, tonight, they stare out opposite
    windows
From inside the Yellow night cab

I Want You to Hate this Poem

I want you to hate this poem

I want you to ignore me
Tell me to "Get off the stage!"
Throw shit at me, throw basura,
Throw bloated up pigeon carcasses

I want you to revile me
    And stalk me, post shit on the Internet
    about me
I want to be cursed in your Churches
And welcomed in your slums

I do not write for the good people;

Home Owners Associations
Not for the tenured

Not for the Solidly Middle Class

I want you to hate this poem
Pretty girls, wearing crosses around your
    necks,
I do NOT want your pussy
I want you to be offended that
I mentioned the fact

That you have a pussy

I want to be told to never read here again
I want to leave this place penniless
    tonight…

  And with scars

I want you to try
Try with all your displeasure
All your Law
All of your God

To kill me

I want you to hate this poem
I am not here to enlighten you
I am not here to curry favor

To repeat the things you think you need
to hear

That is not

Why I am here

Late Sunday Afternoons and Faithlessness

Late
Sunday
Afternoons;
The questions come
Before the sun sets
Western skies, still so far

Spring
Renews
Wild Flowers
Huicache thorns bloom
Wind dies down with dusk
Late Sunday Afternoons

Ask
Listen
All answers,
No longer true

While remembering
The innocence of Faith

French-Pressed Coffee

She gave me the gift of
French-pressed coffee
Still at that stage,
Getting to know each other
Reaching, slightly past the familiar
Aching for requited relief

French Press method is
Zen for Coffee
The perfect combination of
Activity and Patience
Doing and Not Doing,
A watched pot does, indeed, boil

But, it is the unexpected
That we crave
    and fear
And, in time,

Nestle in our palm
And recline with
To savor
Like French Pressed Coffee

Van Horn Rest Stop

I-10

My 10

Through San Antonio from the East

San Antonio of married fights

And west side Basic training Air Force flights

Through Kerrville

Limestone

Hill Country

Ozona, Junction, Sonora

And more

I-10

My 10

On a rainy desert day

Stopping in Fort Stockton

Clinging to Central Time

Speeding straight past Balmohorea

The water's everywhere today

I-10

My 10

I thought I saw Dean Moriarty

With a duffel bag

Spare-changing at the Van Horn piss stop

He appeared as a homeless Vet,

Still out on the road

Eyes shifty and cold

I slipped him a 20

Cause I've been there before

Along I-10

My 10

We've all down that road in the rain

But it's I-10

My 10

That brings me home again

The Tears of Texas

The pained tears of Texas flow
Sorrows run through remote desert and
scrub brush
The Pecos, Colorado, the Brazos

The joyous tears of Texas smile upon
Limestone, mesquite, and sand dunes
The Guadalupe, Red, the Nueces

The Rio Grande…once, so brave

The tears of Texas nourish and feed
Our hungry land
On their way back

To the sea

Schrödinger's Cat

She is releasing

A poem from a pen that she claims
   will not write

In an Indian restaurant

2000 miles away

And I am sitting in Texas

Like Schrödinger's cat

With razor-wire and shot guns

 And a beaker of State-issued
   cyanide

On its way to the floor

Waiting

Waiting for the future to offer

Another chance at the past

Truth has become a label

For popular approval

Binary gravity crushes everyone, if
    we are worthy at all

Would what has already been, exist

If I were not recalling it now?

If you were not looking past the
regret

In the lines around my eyes?

She knows best, a shadow me,

Constructed from yesterday's
    tomorrows and dreams

Maybe, she's already opened that
    door

  Seen my small feline body expired
    on the floor

Or maybe I'm still there, pawing at
    the latch

Ready to claw and spit and scratch
    like Schrodinger's cat

Then, there in Berkeley,

The reading begins

And I sit in Texas

 I sweat, I look over my shoulder

At the past made present, stuck on
    pause;

  and my pen works perfectly

sending my now

to the future
Waiting for the past to be sent back…

Like Schrödinger's cat.

What is Beat, Anyway?

It's still out there
You know…
On The Road

If you have the eyes to find it
    and if you listen with an ear for futility

It's in the turn lanes
Of the city streets
It's in donut shops in mid-afternoon
In bars right next to nail salons
In bail bond agents' waiting rooms
Laundromats always make me
Think of Ginsberg
    and Alan Oak
That long walk to the highway
After they let you out of Del Valle Jail

It's the cats crowding the dumpster
Behind the Taco Bell
It's what churches and temples

Have always promised
It's a paperback library
Started by GI's somewhere
Surrounded by sandbags

It's that same, sad, sweater

You've worn for decades,
Bought at a thrift store
Someplace that it snowed

It's not trusting mirrors any longer
It's learning that lies
Have always been here
They are aboriginal in our DNA,
Twisted
Terrors behind every freedom
Liberty and anonymity are the greatest
dangers
      and
The only paths to Desolation

The Lovelorn and The Buddhists

Love has been called the most exquisite
    form of self destruction
The lovelorn and the Buddhists agree on
    this point
If it's really love

The last week of the year
Christmas is gone

And I cannot make excuses anymore

Demons and doubts
Wrestle by the fire
Like Rottweiler puppies

And, down here in Texas
Not even the cold can be counted on

That's Desolation, man

When winter won't come
To excuse the chill in my bones
So I light out, onto the highway

Always the highway
In late December
With the lovelorn and the Buddhists

Wheeler Peak Echoes

*written New Year's Eve 1999, Taos, NM

I want to take the Walt Whitman exit
    from this road-novel America
Show me to the dream
    that is promised by rural creeks and
Streams

I need to feel the sun, hot upon my naked
    flesh
beside the Gulf again, humid
    as I share it with an as yet unmet
Beloved

I want the divide between creation and
    engineering
To tumble like towers
Like ivory towers struck head-on
By the gypsy power
Of natural light...
SUPERnatural darkness
The reflection of Orion in a lunar eclipse

I want the concrete and blacktop parallels
    of West Texas oilfields
To be cultivated with milo and grazed by
    antelope
And the bridges torn down
    and the cables unstrung
And the airports burned to ash on the
    ground
And the ships to be scuttled

The traffic noise muffled
The fields returned for the insects to farm

I want to stand in one place
    and know:
THIS IS IT
Pure, Intended,
Nature Incarnate
To wake up in the morning...
To wake up in my senses
America, free again
    no prisons, no fences

Wheeler Peak echoes in memories haunt
Tucson sunsets,
Golden Gate fogs...

Poetry stripped to Desolate Bones
Zen Bones
No more compelled to rattle around

Burroughs in the Back

For a long, damned run there

I could have sworn

That it was Billy Burroughs- hitchhiker
Riding stoned in my backseat
A faint, rear-view, reflection
Of decades old cologne

But, when I looked again
It was just a grease stain
On my mirror
And, I remembered

I now drive a pickup-truck
And haven't picked up a hitchhiker
In years...

Counting Cards

Science and Religion; equally flawed
poles on an absolute falsehood

When pushed hard enough, even
mathematics crumble in futility

Humility

Is admitting

That there is no value, no values

The multiverse always appears

At the end of our calculations, at the end
of our prayers

Finite nature is a lie

Our minds reflect the multiverse, our
bodies were merely created in some god's
    image

If there can be an "Everywhere",

There can be an "Every When"

Big Bang theory explains it all,

Except for the "Why"

The Universe is a bubble in an infinite
    bubble bath

Reality is merely the science of
    likelihood
Approximations and calculated risk

Theology is counting cards at the
    grandest table

It is really worth thinking about,

As fields of bluebonnets and primrose
    bloom?

Death Sits

Death sits with me on my bedside
She sits and we talk of the smallest of
    things
In the bedroom of my 100 year old home

There is no Faith after death, she tells me
No yearning, no dread
No loss, no fear, no fear of loss
Death is no tempest nor torrent,
Though I knew her to be like that once

But, she will not use words like "Peace"
    or "Serene"
She tells me it is almost like a dream, but
    not entirely
And she hastens me back to sleep

Home Fire

Fire
Home fire
Long denied
Calling me back
To South Texas roots
Soul fire, Brush fire, Home fire

Years
Decades
Out of touch
Not keeping score
Plumes of smoke drifting
Unseen fires smoldering

Flames
Dancing
Elements

Released from form
Mixing with the night
Shining bright, Glowing heat

I Did Not Go Looking for This

I did not go looking for this!
It found me, stalked me, seduced me,
Swung open the passenger door in front
    of the San Antonio Greyhound station
And jumped right in
It bled red onto my cluttered floorboard
And drank the last of my travelling wine.

I did not go looking for this.
When I weighed anchor in the mist
On a God-less Mogadishu night,
The mujahedeen punk-ass hid itself
And played spades in the chain-locker
    until the storm-winds picked up.

It jumped out at me, horny and afraid,
From an alley in the Tenderloin
Lecherous tongue and demon hard cock,

hash-stained fingers and a needle in its
    shriveling arm
It left saliva on my cheek
And salvia stains in my homeless
    dungarees .

I did not go looking for this!
I just knew how to find it
I followed the sound that hunger makes in
    the morning
Because, that tune has soul...
And I'd ride five thousand miles EASY,
    when I'm in the mood for SOUL....

You Can't Be Beat No More

…And there's this sack-of-shit hipster
   poet
Sitting near the stage with his Westlake
Hills girlfriend
Waiting for his turn at the Open Mic
So that he can spout his shit and leave

   (while others read)

Smoking the most expensive cigarettes he
   could find, and drinking
 Pabst from a can

You can't be beat anymore, no
They just won't let you, he says
With a Fuck-bomb and a sneer
You can't be beat no more, Man
You can't hitch-hike like Kerouac
There are crazies out there

You can't get stoned and zoned like
Kesey, Man
They test you now, you know
And the chicks don't dig it when you
    fuck like
Corso fucked
You just can't be beat no more, Man
They won't LET YOU, Man

And I wonder; did he set the alarm on his
    car
Before he came into the bar?
'Cause this Cat is right…

He'll never be Beat

I Do Not Love Your Jesus

I do not think that I love your Jesus
That is,
I'm pretty sure that we've never met
I mean,
That one summer, those two weeks
At Baylor University

We washed small town, Texas, cars for a
    year
To raise the cash to go

As a 14 year old
They made us cry
They showed us videos of preachers with
    hideous scars
Burn scars, and told us that we would
Burn forever unless we said that we
    believed

So, we did…say that we believed

And long, repetitive, chant-like songs
Were sung…
 Praise choruses, over and over
Oxygen deprivation always feels like
    grace

I know your fear
I know your stone and marble columns

I even know your ripe and well groomed
    daughters,
Sent away to find salvation at Baylor
University in the summer

But, I am not sure that I ever knew your
    Jesus
I'm fairly certain that he has never known
    me

I'm not saying that I hate your Jesus
Because we've never really met
But, you tell me that the two of you are

very close
That you love him, so

I'll respect your relationship
And leave you both alone

If I ever see your Jesus, here,
Out on the road

Overnight, Warming Shelter; Victoria, Texas

Picking up poems
Off of the floor
At the overnight
Warming shelter

Freezing in south Texas
Bitter, post-election November
A week away from Thanksgiving
Awake, tending coffee pots

Refugees from the local atmosphere
Natural forces drove us here

Exiles from the cold

Pase, Señor (White Privilege)

It is nine forty nine in the evening
And the gin kicks in
Alone, in a hotel room
    not far from the Mexican border
And I have not yet
Shed my Caucasian privilege

Bass notes from the Tropicana Club
Mariachi Wednesday
The music is pumping,
It is raining in early November
And I have still
    not lost my Anglo privilege

I pass through the check points, Clean
Never sent to secondary screening
Because of my skin
Never asked to
"Get out of the vehicle please",
Because of my last name
Rarely even asked the one question
Everyone is supposed to be asked

Even slightly buzzed
From a weekend of poetry,
I still retain my white race advantage

Even in prison, as likely as not,
I would be chosen to "supervise"
A work detail
Or push a lightweight dust mop
Over air conditioned floors
Even when homeless,
I could shoplift at will,
No store detectives following me
Minimum sentences, a million second
    chances
Even when they took my ID in Santa Fe
And wouldn't give it back
My European privilege let me sneak out
    of town

I can not apologize for my privilege,
The things others feel, when they see

The
Big
White
Boy

Hiding in Mexico,
I could drink on the plaza
Until after midnight.
Las botellas chingonas, Carta y Lager
Pero, los indios were not allowed,
And, could be arrested on sight

I do not hide from my privilege;
I know that it's there
I do not seek it nor deserve it;
I know it's not fair
I do not embrace it, as it clings to me
With the cement of conquistador armies
White privilege, muy fácilmente,
Becomes gringo guilt
And shame

But, I am not ashamed of myself

I am ashamed for those that look at me,
And wave me ahead of them,
In check out lines at the H.E. B. in
Edinburg;

"Pase, Señor"....When a checker opens a
   fresh checkout line

And I have two bottles of wine and a six-
   pack of tall-boys
While they have a SNAP benefits card
   and fideo noodles.

Pase, Señor.

Lions of Summer

It is summer again,
That humid afternoon violence returns

Texas is harsh to a 40 year old,
    peeling back decades
Like a sunburned skin slough
To when lions sought shade
Under the wings of airlifters
    and human clavicles
Grew bleached by the sun

Lions will not hurt you
In the light of day,
If you do not force them
From their shade

They prefer to hunt at night, together
There is no billet for a solitary lion
    back here on these heated,
 Lone-Star, plains

Just things left best undisturbed,
    decades ago,

In African shade.

I Was Dreaming, Again, of Iraq

The Ambien wears off
And, it's not the same as waking up
I am rock hard in a half dream
We had stopped her at a checkpoint
And, despite her fear and anger
This chick is hot, with a harbinger of lust
And, yeah…that was the dream

Using the muzzle of that M4 carbine
To penetrate, take, possess- to occupy
Her black haired, native, cunt
While a female NCO I had met
    somewhere
Forces her uncovered face into her wet,
    well trimmed, gash
And, we mock her

But this Haji-chick knows
Just what to do
And, through tears now

Is forcing herself back on the condom-
    covered muzzle
She moans and sighs
Around the oral attentions between
    blonde American thighs

Hijab, ripped; large, yet still firm. breasts
The color of Persian moonlight, pant
    faster and faster
The women climax at the same time

Daughters of Lilith, not far from the
    original Garden
While I am impotent without that weapon
Denied of any knowing that does not
    come through force

Soldiers should behave in certain ways,
And do soldierly things
She regains her modest clothes,

And turns to give us both a parting kiss
We have been humans, guttural and
    depraved
Melting tools of hate and killing into
    pools of lust
Sins, still deadly
Reveling in our lost natures

And, I am left rock hard
As the Ambien wears off

House of Cards

...and just now I have the feeling

That the stars have lost their meaning

And eternal things

   are phantoms now, laughing in the wind

I've walked the scorching desert

And I've sailed the raging sea

But in the end, I know it's all the same

  for folks like you and me

And just now, I remember

  waking from a dream

A place in Marin County and tall, tall, trees so green

It's buyer's remorse, I find

  for the torches I had to buy

To burn the bridges of mirror and smoke

 stumblin' towards the light

And just now, I can't look forward to

 a golden road at all

I guess every house of cards we build

 is gonna have to fall

Like a cowboy rodeo rider, on an angry, bucking bronc -

I just can't take it slow, and the only way to make it stop

Is to let go holding of the reins- and simply take the ride

And just now, I stand aside, amazed

at how we've both survived

And just now, I feel, it's all the same

with every break of day

That maybe it could be better somehow

out there by the Bay

But the headlights on the highway

can blind you to the truth

Just like bus stop benches, soup-line food,

 and rot-gut 80 proof

And just now, I have the feeling (that)

It's not that bad at all

And that every house of cards we build

 is gonna have to fall...

If I Came to Your Door

If I came to your door, scared and alone
Would you help me?

If I arrived in the dead of night,
With nothing but scars on my back,
Would you rip your laundry into
    bandages for me?

If the tears from my cheeks would fill the
Rio Grande River,
The Nile River, The Jordan River;
Would my sorrows be enough
To reach you?

If I came to you, in your church,
Asking for one day of peace and freedom,
Would you prosecute me?
While praying for those sheltered within
    your walls?

If I came to you, speaking a strange
    tongue,
Would we laugh and smoke and dine
    together,
Sharing common tastes?

If I came to you,
Without bag, without horse, without cart,
Would you shoulder your rifle aimed at
    my heart?

To deny a hope, to rage against fate,
May be the quickest way to teach a child
    hate.

You have cast aside diamonds, and
    rubies, and teachings so wise;

Stealing the dreams from ancient, brown,
    eyes

Only savage nobles on la frontera today,
And nothing more
If I came to your door.

Water, Blood

The border is not chain link and wire

Not concrete, steel, or guns

It is the water that flows from snow melt
And that nurtures sandia vines in the
    fields

It is blood of the Earth

Sangre de gente

Spilled blood, life blood,

Family and Faith

The border is not history

It is hope

It is not yesterday
It is today

Blood Moon

I heard there was gonna be a Blood Moon

I stocked up on gauze and bandages
The Christians were buying ammunition
    and padlocks
Talkin' bout their Prophet's return

I wondered, has this Moon been typed
    and cross-matched?
How do we avoid infection?
Or,
Is Moon blood Universal Blood?

This Blood Moon.

Roadtrip (Paying for the Gas)

A tattered copy of "Sirens of Titan"
    is chosen over bad motel TV
At the start of a five state road-trip

Coffee, sleeping pills and truck stops
    four dollar gasoline
Seems all too much to spend for poetry
And words of witness shouted into the
    irrelevant abyss

Our Nation is still a large, large place
    every bit a big as it seems
When you step away from diplo-speak;
War on drugs, red state/blue state scenes

Miles seem longer and horizons farther
    once you're west of Abilene

Soaring over landscapes at 30 thousand
    feet
Like invading armies, to drop from the air

Can not compare to time and investment
Involved in the task of driving there

Coastal Plains turn into desert
Like the dryness that sometimes
    desiccates my soul

But climbing ever higher, shifts things
    greener
Not through rain or storms but elevations

Altitude
Attitude; the angle of approach

Driving on with four wheels firmly
    planted in nothingness
Crossing state lines in the dark
As if they meant something…anything at
all

Roadside poets and alley-cats
Discordant music and pork-pie hats
Superstitious mountains
Rippled nipples peeking from silky
    chemises

Rock shops and cycle cops
Adding air to the left front tire in a
Las Cruces parking lot
Lower Pima County steam-punk truck
    stops

Free speech in Phoenix, confined to an
    alley
History of longevity, and that one
    mother-fucker of a cat
From a Bukowski paper-back
Driving onward, through Maricopa
    darkness
Like Kerouac, with the back-seat packed

Don't give up, Don't give up
Don't cry, Don't die
Don't scream
They'll get you then

And the sun will come up,
If you lose or if you win
Take away the take away
Burn minutes into miles
Like it has always been done
Caffeine, Nicotine
Grass, and desert sand

Sand-stone Arches
Green sheen north of Moab,
Keep going, keep moving
Shiprock, ship-wreck, Colorado line
It just takes time

Time is all you have,
    with the hours of your life

You're only paying for the gas

Jack Kerouac's Smile

It's like Beat women,

Sent off to asylums
Suicides
Of post-war queers

To wake up and discover
That, sometime as I slept
I had rolled over
Onto
And killed
The smallest, grey, kitten

So, I find a plastic bag
And slip on house-shoes
To go out to the dumpster

Like the smile
That Jack kept ready
For the women that Neal would leave
    behind

Of Steering Wheels and Bulldogs

He lays
On the
Passenger side
Floor board
As the
Pronghorn
Antelope
Sun rises,
Staining F-150
Rear windshield
Glass
Somewhere
Just outside
Raton

Heading north and west,
Gary Snyder
Bulldog
Eyes
Look up
And catch mine

I tease him, asking, out loud

"Where are we, Buddy?
Where are we, Boy?"

Like
Somehow
I know things
His canine mind
Can't capture

Yet
From somewhere
So far off and far away,
That even words
Are vain,
Where life and love
Hold no form

Comes his mystical, sensible,
Hobo Zen,
Answer;

"Together,
Together is where we are.

Just drive,
      motherfucker,
            Drive…"

AUTHOR'S NOTE:

I want to express my most sincere
gratitude to Chuck Taylor and
Christopher Carmona of Slough Press for
bringing this collection to light. It has
been an honor to work with and get to
know them both over the last several
years.

After self publishing two previous poetry
collections, reading at a hundred or more
open mic events across this massive state,
and submitting poems and stories to
journals, 'zines, and anthologies until my
finger tips grew calloused and my eyes
burned, this collection is the realization of
a dream that never died.

Some of the poems included in this
collection date back to the mid 1990's…a
few were written earlier this year. This

collection is the work product of two wars, two Texas prison sentences, and a few hitches in county jails.

This book was written with the kind of ink that only flows from divorces, empty Bourbon bottles, and the smell of jet fuel.

Highway rest areas and hurricanes helped write these poems, as did food served on plastic trays at psychiatric hospitals.

These poems are the written remains of decades, and their story is not yet complete.

Keep writing, keep reading and keep
finding a way to turn reality into
truth…your truth.
I will see you out there, in the reflections
of barroom mirrors and highway signs.

-PW Covington, Yoakum, Texas,
Summer, 2015

ABOUT THE AUTHOR

Photo by Leslie Anne Jensen

PW Covington was born in Victorville,
California in 1974. Born into a military
family, Covington moved often as

a child before his family settled in the south Texas town of Cuero, just before he started high school. After four semesters at Victoria College, he enlisted in the United States Air Force, where he served with the 2nd Mobile Aerial Port Squadron, deploying to both southwest Asia and Somalia in his duty as an Air Transportation Specialist.

Covington began writing poetry after leaving the Air Force, during a period of homeless wandering that took him to the Bay Area of California, cities across the southwestern US, and Mexico's Copper Canyon region.

He has worked as a day laborer, a merchant mariner, a zookeeper, a radio disc jockey, a political campaign staffer, a steel worker, as ground crew for a major US airline, a back-country canyon guide, a truck driver, and as a mental health peer counselor, among other endeavors.

PW Covington has served time in Texas jails and prisons, and has written extensively about those experiences.

His work has been included in both underground, independent, 'zines and journals published by academic institutions such as University of Texas Pan American, Our Lady of the Lake University, and South Texas College.

Covington was nominated for a Pushcart Prize for his flash fiction piece "*Day Sleeper*" in 2013.

More information about the writer can be found online at www.PWCovington.com .

"Family Housing" was previously published by Virgogray Press, *Carcinogenic Poetry*, Aug 2014

"Don't Give it a Name" was previously published in the collection *I Did Not Go Looking for This*.

"DeWitt County" was previously published by *Harbinger Asylum*.

"Short Final" was previously published in the collection *I Did Not Go Looking For This* and by Penhall Publishing, *Not Dead Yet*.

"It Was Not Sacrifice" was previously published in the collection *I Did Not Go Looking for This*.

"The Last Time that the World Ended" has been previously published by Our Lady of the Lake University, *The Thing Itself 2014,* Penhall Publishing, *Not Dead Yet*, and South Texas College, *Interstice 2014*.

"The Smoke Also Rises" was previously published in the collection *I Did Not Go Looking For This*

."Recidivists" was previously published by Penhall Publishing, *Not Dead Yet* and Stout City's 'zine, *Come and Take It*.

"PTSD" was previously published in the collections *Like the Prayers of an Infidel* and *I Did Not Go Looking for This*.

"Poems that begin with the Letter I" was previously published by *Your One Phone Call* (UK) and *Mad Swirl*.

"Veterans Assistance Office" was previously published in the collection *I Did Not Go Looking for This.*

"Ode to a Corduroy Coat" was previously published by *Harbinger Asylum.*

"Never Work with Food" was previously published by Virgogray Press,
Carcinogenic Poetry and The Permian
Basin Poetry Society, *beyond 2014.*

"A Few Grains of Sand" was previously published by American Institute of Stress (Jun 2013 *Combat Stress Newsletter*) and in the collection *I Did Not Go Looking for This*

"For Edward Viduarre" was previously published in *Harbinger Asylum.*

"Echo Hotel" was previously published by Rio Grande Valley International Poetry Festival, *Boundless 2014* and South Texas College, *Interstice 2014.*

"Ambrose" was previously published in the collection *I Did Not Go Looking for This* and by South Texas College, *Interstice 2013.*

"Catching a Cab from 26th and Valencia" was previously published by Transcendent Zero Press, *To Hold a Moment Still.*

"I Want You to Hate This Poem" was previously published by Kool Press, *Junkyard Kool.*

"Late Sunday Afternoons and Faithlessness" was previously published by *Harbinger Asylum.*

"French Pressed Coffee" was previously published by *Harbinger Asylum.*

"Van Horn rest Stop" was previously published by The Permian Basin Poetry Society, *beyond 2014.*

"Schrödinger's Cat " was previously published in the collection *Collapsed Lexicon,* Kool Press

"Wheeler Peak Echoes" was previously published in the collection *I Did Not Go Looking for This.*

"Counting Cards" was previously Published by *Harbinger Asylum.*

"Death Sits" was previously published by *Harbinger Asylum.*

"Home Fire" was previously published by Permian Basin Poetry Society, *beyond 2014.*

"I Did Not Go Looking for This" was previously published by South Texas College, *Interstice 2013* and in the collection *I Did Not Go Looking for This.*

"You Can't be Beat No More" was previously published by Lamar University Press, *Beatest State in the Union.*

"Overnight, Warming Shelter; Victoria, Texas" was previously published by Transcendent Zero Press, *To Hold a Moment Still*

"Pase, Señor (White Privilege) " was previously published by South Texas College, *Interstice 2014.*

"Lions of Summer" was previously published by University of Texas Pan-American, *riverSedge 2014.*

"If I Came to Your Door" was published in *The Border Crossed Us (an anthology to end apartheid),* by VAGABOND and *Interstice 2015* by South Texas College.

"Water, Blood" was previously published by Virgogray Press, *Carcinogenic Poetry.*

"Roadtrip (Paying for the Gas)" was previously published in the collection I *Did Not Go Looking for This.*

"Jack Kerouac's Smile" was first published by Entropy Magazine's *Final Poem Project.*

"Of Steering Wheels and Bulldogs" was first published by *Dead Snakes Journal.*

www.ingramcontent.com/pod-product-compliance
Lightning Source LLC
Chambersburg PA
CBHW060243050426
42448CB00009B/1569